AI for Disaster Recovery

Planning, Mitigation, and Response

Table of Contents

Chapter 1. Introduction

Special Report: AI for Disaster Recovery - Planning, Mitigation, and Response

In an era where natural and man-made disasters seem to be an inevitable part of our lives, robust and efficient disaster recovery mechanisms are of utmost importance. How about we use the power of Artificial Intelligence to enhance our preparedness, and response mechanisms? Sounds a bit technical, but fret not, because this special report titled "AI for Disaster Recovery: Planning, Mitigation, and Response" aims to enlighten your journey into this fascinating blend of technology and public safety. The report is crafted in a straightforward, down-to-earth manner that decodes complexities of AI and highlights how it can be a game-changer in disaster recovery efforts. Whether you're a public policy maker, a business leader, or an inquisitive reader, this comprehensive special report will provide you with insightful and practical knowledge, thus empowering you to shape the future of disaster management in an AI-driven world. Take a dive into this critical exploration of artificial intelligence – we promise this reads more like an intriguing everyday-tech story than a intimidating tech manual.

Chapter 2. Understanding Disasters and their implications

Natural or man-made disasters inevitably alter the course of humanity. This life-altering impact may scale from economic losses to irreversible environmental destruction, and unfortunately, loss of life. To better comprehend the profound influence these disastrous events have on our world, we first must understand the nature and implications of disasters comprehensively.

2.1. Dissecting the Term Disaster

When we deem an event as a 'disaster,' it usually signifies a sudden, unfortunate event that leads to significant material, economic, or environmental damage, and often, loss of life. Typically, these are unforeseen incidents that result in significant disruption and destruction in the lives of those affected. From a deluge of rain causing urban flooding to an unexpected earthquake shaking the root of civilizations, disasters frequently originate from natural phenomena. They can also derive from human-made occurrences like nuclear accidents or oil spills, leading to environmental and human tragedies.

Disasters are usually characterized by the scale of their impact. It is pertinent to mention that the term is often used when these catastrophic events occur in areas where humans inhabit. This specificity is crucial because it's not just the occurrence of these devastating events that matter, but also their severity and the vulnerability of the affected area.

2.2. A Closer Look at Different Types of Disasters

Broadly speaking, disasters are either natural or man-made. Natural disasters are primarily due to adverse environmental phenomena and include events such as earthquakes, volcanic eruptions, tsunamis, floods, hurricanes, and droughts. Natural disasters like these are generally beyond human control.

Conversely, man-made disasters can often be a result of human negligence, error, or intent. These include industrial accidents, oil spills, transport accidents, fires, technological failures, or terror attacks. While some man-made disasters are intentional, others, like Chernobyl's nuclear disaster, are the effect of human error combined with technological and system failure.

Now that we have discerned the basic types, let's delve deeper into the significant features, consequences, and challenges related to these two categories.

2.3. The Underlying Features and Consequences of Natural Disasters

Natural disasters and their implications remain a significant concern worldwide, causing immense human suffering and damage to the natural and built environments. They often occur with incredible force and unleash an astronomical amount of energy. Earthquakes, tornadoes, and tsunamis are events caused by tectonic movements within the Earth's crust, which can have devastating immediate responses and long-lasting impact.

Floods, a frequent natural disaster, result from excessive rainfall within a short period. This uncontrolled water can cause landslides, transportation disruption, and significant damage to buildings and infrastructure. In the long-term, it can lead to soil erosion, water pollution, and crop failure.

Droughts are another insidious form of natural disaster. They develop over an extended period and can lead to widespread famine, dehydration, and wildfires causing extensive material damage and loss of life. Similarly, excessive heat can lead to heatwaves, causing hyperthermia and dehydration and increasing mortality rates, particularly among vulnerable populations.

These disasters, hence, can have immediate to long-term implications ranging from physical destruction and loss of life to societal, economic, and environmental impacts. It is the subsequent cascading effects of these events that transform them from natural phenomena to disasters.

2.4. Unpacking the Consequences of Man-Made Disasters

Man-made disasters, often caused by a failure of systems created by humans, signify the dark side of technological and industrial progress. Many of these are accidents resulting from negligence or lack of regulations. Industrial disasters, such as those at Bhopal in India and Chernobyl in Ukraine, have demonstrated the potential for catastrophic impact, involving substantial loss of life and long-lasting environmental damage.

Another common type of man-made disaster is transportation accidents. Whether on land, in the air, or at sea, these accidents can result in significant harm and are frequently due to mechanical failures or human error.

Finally, man-made disasters can also be intentional, such as acts of terrorism or warfare, which deliberately and violently disrupt societies, causing death, destruction, and panic.

Just like natural disasters, man-made disasters too have both immediate and long-term effects. They can lead to material damage and loss of life, along with profound psychological impacts on survivors and societies. The loss of infrastructure can weaken economies, and the environmental fallout from disasters like nuclear or chemical accidents can take years, if not decades, to remediate.

In the next phase, having a clear understanding of disasters and their implications, we can propound systems and strategies powered by AI for effective disaster management. Better comprehension of the problem equips us optimally to implement solution-based approaches, leveraging technology for disaster preparedness, mitigation, and recovery.

Chapter 3. Introducing Artificial Intelligence: A Simplified Overview

Although Artificial Intelligence (AI) often appears immersed in jargon and complex concepts, at its core, it is simply about mimicking and replicating human intelligence processes through machines, especially computer systems.

These processes include machine learning, where systems learn and improve from experience, natural language processing which allows them to understand and interact using human language, and cognitive computing that simulates human thought processes in a computerized model.

3.1. The Origin and Evolution of AI

Artificial Intelligence as a concept is not new. Early mathematicians and inventors, as far back as the Greek antiquity, sought to create mechanical devices with capabilities to replicate human behavior. However, it was not until 1956, during a conference at Dartmouth College, the term "Artificial Intelligence" was coined. The conference saw scientists from various fields set out to find if machines could simulate any aspect of intelligence, raising the curtains for what we now think of as AI.

Following this, the 1960s and 1970s saw AI research funded by the Defense Advanced Research Projects Agency (DARPA), including projects focused on problem-solving, linguistic theory, and even simulating basic forms of human intelligence.

As we entered the 1980s and 1990s, AI marked its place in the commercial market, with companies tapping into its potential to optimize operations, enhance customer service, and unearth insights from data. However, despite all the advancements, AI systems were still largely rule-based and lacked the capability to learn from their experiences.

This concept of learning from experience was later incorporated in the 2000s, marking the evolution of machine learning. Since then, AI has transformed dramatically, fueled by massive increases in data volume and computational power. Today, not only do AI systems learn from data, but their intelligence also evolves over time, enabling them to improve their outcomes and make more accurate predictions.

3.2. Components of AI

Understanding the different components of AI is key to comprehending its full scope and potential. Here we disentangle 3 major components of AI:

1. Natural Language Processing (NLP): The ability of an AI system to understand and interact in human language. It forms the basis of voice assistants like Siri and Alexa.

2. Machine Learning (ML): This refers to the ability of AI systems to learn from experience and data, improving their performance over time. Machine Learning underpins recommendation algorithms used by services such as Netflix or YouTube.

3. Cognitive Computing: A complex component that aims to mimic human thought processes in a computerized model. It forms the base for more advanced systems.

3.3. How AI Works

In essence, AI works by ingesting massive amounts of data, gleaning patterns from this data, and then using these patterns to make predictions. This process is accomplished using a variety of techniques:

1. Data Collection: AI systems require massive amounts of data to understand and learn from patterns. Data can be collected from many sources like databases, online feeds, sensors, among others.

2. Data Preparation: The collected data is then cleaned, organized, and transformed into a format that can be used by AI algorithms.

3. Algorithm Selection: Appropriate learning algorithms are selected based on the problem at hand and the available data.

4. Training and Testing: The AI models are then trained using the prepared data and subsequently tested to evaluate their performance.

As the models ingest more data over time, they continue to refine their understanding, thus improving their future predictions and performance.

In sum, AI revolves around the concept of enabling machines to mimic human intelligence, learn from experiences and improve over time. Its current applications range from virtual personal assistants to self-driving cars and it continues to advance, marking its footprint across various industries.

3.4. AI in the Real World

From Google's search engine algorithms to Amazon's product recommendations, AI has permeated into our everyday lives. The technology is especially transformative in sectors like healthcare, finance, and transportation. For example, AI algorithms are aiding doctors in diagnosing diseases, predicting patient risks, and personalizing treatment plans. In finance, AI is streamlining processes like fraud detection, risk management, and customer service. As for transportation, the advent of AI-powered autonomous vehicles is set to revolutionize personal and commercial transportation.

3.5. Future of AI

The future of AI carries a promise of unprecedented possibilities. Continued advancements in machine learning algorithms, coupled with improvements in data collection and processing, are set to unlock new frontiers for AI. Promising areas include enhanced decision-making capabilities, real-time speech translation, advanced automation, and solutions to complex global challenges.

From the perspective of disaster recovery, these advancements in artificial intelligence could significantly transform planning, mitigation, and response mechanisms. For instance, AI algorithms can enhance forecasting accuracy, inform risk assessments, drive efficient resource allocation, and improve communication during recovery operations.

As we continue to embrace AI, a note of caution is in order: while AI offers immense potential, its ethical use and implications on privacy, jobs, and societal norms also warrant careful considerations. That said, if navigated thoughtfully, AI has the potential to reshape our collective future in profound and beneficial ways.

In the following chapters, we shall delve into the practicalities of leveraging AI for disaster recovery. We shall explore how concepts, such as machine learning, can inform disaster planning, identify potential risks and areas of vulnerabilities, guide in the allocation of resources during a disaster, and finally, aid in coordinating a swift and efficient recovery.

Chapter 4. The Role of AI in Disaster Risk Assessment

Ever since the advent of technology, risk assessment has been a crucial part of disaster management. Fundamentally, it pertains to the identification and evaluation of risks and uncertainties associated with hazards that can lead to disasters. Now, with Artificial Intelligence entering the arena, the landscape for this critical task has considerably evolved.

4.1. AI-Enabled Disaster Risk Identification

Risk identification, in conventional terms, is about figuring out what could go wrong. Generally, it relies on historical data and on-the-ground assessments. The integration of AI, though, has opened avenues for a much more comprehensive and incisive risk identification.

AI systems, when fed with humongous amounts of past data, can draw patterns and deduce correlations that human minds generally cannot fathom. Deep learning algorithms, a subset of AI, are now capable of identifying potential disaster zones, even in the absence of any notable human intervention. They do so by analyzing patterns found in satellite imagery, geospatial data, and relevant historical records.

For instance, AI can identify areas prone to floods during a cyclone by cross-referencing storm trajectories and regional rainfall data with topographic, soil, and hydrographic information. Similarly, forest fires, often instigated by abnormally high temperature, drought conditions, and gusty winds, can be anticipated in advance by AI systems monitoring weather patterns and historical occurrences.

4.2. AI-Driven Disaster Risk Evaluation

Once the risks are identified, evaluating their potential impact becomes a sine qua non. Traditionally, disaster managers have relied on rule-based systems, and to some extent, statistical models, to estimate the possible damage and the associated economic costs.

AI, with its ability to learn and improve over time, holds the potential to supersede these traditional methods. Machine learning algorithms can model complex situations, with myriad variables influencing disaster outcomes, thereby providing a more sophisticated understanding.

Take, for instance, a flash flood --- a whirl of geological, atmospheric, and hydrological elements manifesting in an unforeseen manner. Evaluating flood risk would necessitate an understanding of topography, local history of rainfall intensity, rate of urbanization, soil saturation levels, and even encroachments on water bodies. Machine learning models can integrate and interrogate these multiple datasets, predicting outcomes such as flood severity, the extent of the flood, and the consequent loss of property and life.

4.3. AI for Early Warning and Alert Systems

Accurate early warning systems can significantly improve risk mitigation and disaster response planning. AI plays a pivotal role in this regard. AI applications in implementing early warning systems include predictive analysis, automated threat detection, and swift dissemination of warnings.

Several meteorological departments, research institutions, and tech companies have developed AI-based models, capable of predicting severe weather events and issuing early warnings. Google's AI firm, DeepMind, has been working on advanced machine learning models to predict rainfall up to several hours in advance using high-resolution radar data.

For rapid and effective threat detection, AI models are being trained to process satellite imagery data in real-time. NASA's AI4Mars project uses AI to interpret high-resolution images taken from Mars rovers for detecting threats such as sandstorms or toxic geological conditions.

4.4. Disaster Impact Projection using AI

AI technologies also allow us to project disaster effects concerning casualties, economic losses, and social disruptions. For example, social impact forecasting models are being designed to anticipate the impact of a disaster on vulnerable populations. They use social, demographic, and economic data to predict patterns of displacement, strain on community resources, and even potential civil unrest in the wake of a disaster.

Such comprehensive forecasts can lead to more nuanced disaster management strategies, including advanced evacuation plans, better aid distribution management, and targeted relief efforts.

4.5. AI in Mitigation Planning

Integrating AI in disaster risk assessment can go a long way in formulating actionable mitigation plans. As AI models predict disaster scenarios with increasing accuracy, planning authorities can use these projections to devise optimal directions for emergency response resources, actionable evacuation routes, and locations for relief centers.

Collaborating with Geo-AI systems, municipal and regional authorities can determine which infrastructures are especially vulnerable in the event of a disaster. This can inform better building regulations, zoning laws, and infrastructure development strategies.

AI, coupled with strong data infrastructure and cutting-edge algorithms, is transforming the way we assess, prepare, and plan for disasters. By harnessing its potential, we can prioritize the safety and well-being of communities at risk and develop resilience in the face of looming threats.

Chapter 5. AI for Disaster Planning: Preparing for the Inevitable

One fundamental adage is that prevention is always better than cure. In the context of disaster management, that means ample planning and preparation. As we move into a technologically advanced era, AI has a crucial role to play in disaster planning.

5.1. AI in Risk Assessment and Disaster Prediction

At the heart of disaster planning is risk assessment. It involves analyzing potential hazards, predicting their chances of occurrence, and envisaging their potential impacts. Traditional forms of risk assessment based purely on historical data have numerous limitations. These include changing climate patterns, alterations in landscape, and shifting demographics, which may render the historical data obsolete. AI, with its ability to interpret real-time data and adapt its algorithms based on evolving conditions, can significantly overcome these limitations.

Machine learning (ML), a subset of AI, can analyze years of meteorological, geological and geographical data and model potential disaster scenarios. AI algorithms can not only recognize patterns in data but can also predict future occurrences, effectively warning about catastrophic events. For instance, AI technologies like Google's DeepMind and IBM's Watson have been used to predict rainfall patterns, estimate their impact, and warn about potential floods.

Moreover, AI can process satellite and drone imagery to assess landscape changes indicating potential disaster sites. For example, analyzing patterns of vegetation growth or melting polar ice could alert about impending landslides or floods.

5.2. AI-Enabled Early Warning Systems

Once potential risks are identified, early warning systems become essential in mitigating disaster impacts. AI can significantly enhance the efficiency and effectiveness of these systems. Real-time data can be instantaneously analyzed to provide warnings far quicker than human-based systems could.

AI's capability for natural language processing can understand and interpret social media posts, news reports, and other public data sources. This can help in recognizing emerging threats and spreading information rapidly among communities, thus, improving preparedness levels. AI systems can also directly send warnings to mobile devices in the risk-prone areas detailing the imminent threat and necessary precautions.

Further, AI can simulate potential evacuation procedures, identifying the most efficient routes and processes. This could potentially save countless lives and resources during disasters. In fact, researchers are experimenting with AI-powered drones and robots that can assist rescue operations.

5.3. AI in Infrastructure Planning and Design

AI can also play an important role in long-term disaster planning through smarter infrastructure design and planning. Techniques like generative design, which uses AI to create thousands of design solutions based on specified input parameters, can help build infrastructure capable of withstanding disastrous situations.

For instance, AI can aid in designing buildings that can endure earthquakes, typhoons, or floods, or help plan resilient urban layouts that are flood-resistant. AI systems can simulate numerous disaster scenarios and test the resilience of various infrastructure designs, ultimately selecting the most effective solutions.

AI can also be instrumental in continually monitoring the integrity of existing infrastructure, such as bridges, dams, roads, and buildings. AI-based solutions can process data from sensors placed on these structures to detect anomalies early on, thus enabling preemptive action before disasters occur.

5.4. The Interplay of AI and IoT in Disaster Planning

The Internet of Things (IoT), integrated with AI, can revolutionize disaster planning. IoT devices can collect copious amounts of data about environmental conditions in real-time. AI algorithms, in turn, can process this data for insights into impending disasters.

Moreover, IoT devices can themselves be empowered by AI. Think smart wearable devices that monitor heart rates, blood pressure, and other vital signs of disaster response teams in real-time, thus ensuring their safety. AI can analyze the data from these devices to predict any potential health risks to the responders, improving their safety and efficiency.

5.5. The Future of Disaster Planning with AI

So, what's the future of disaster planning with AI? We've only just begun to tap into the potential of AI in disaster planning. As AI technology evolves, and as we amass more data, the resulting growth in predictive capabilities will likely be enormous.

Challenges, of course, exist. The success of AI relies heavily on the quantity and quality of data. Ensuring data privacy and security is a concern, as well as making the sophisticated AI-driven analytics accessible and understandable to all stakeholders involved in disaster planning. Also, creating AI systems which can adapt to unforeseen scenarios is an intriguing problem.

However, with ongoing advances in AI technology, these challenges are being addressed steadily, and it's clear that AI has an instrumental role to play in future disaster planning efforts. AI isn't going to replace traditional disaster planning; instead, it will enhance it, making our response to disasters quicker, smarter, and ultimately, more effective.

In conclusion, whether the inevitable disaster is natural or man-made, the adoption of AI can revolutionize our preparedness for it, transforming the grim scenario into a story of resilience and recovery thanks to the power of future-ready technology. AI involvement in disaster planning is not just a theoretical concept but a practical solution to an age-old problem, one that can make a significant difference in saving lives, resources, and time. The future of disaster planning and, indeed, disaster management, will undeniably be smarter, quicker, and more efficient with AI. Now, that is a future we should all plan and prepare for.

Chapter 6. Enhanced Disaster Detection using AI

Artificial intelligence (AI) has revolutionized the way we live and work, and its potentials in disaster detection and mitigation are no exception. Historically, disaster detection has relied on somewhat traditional tools such as GIS mapping or satellite imagery. Now, AI is altering the way we anticipate and respond to calamities by providing an early warning, detecting patterns, and simplifying disaster response and recovery efforts. From natural disasters like wildfire, floods, and earthquakes to human-made disasters like industrial accidents, AI can make all the difference in saving lives, reducing damage, and facilitating faster recovery.

6.1. AI-enabled Early Warning Systems

Traditionally, disaster early warning systems (EWS) involved significant human intervention and were prone to error. In contrast, AI-powered EWS can process data from various sources, analyze it, and predict potential threats within a matter of seconds. One such example is the utilization of machine learning in predicting forest fires. AI algorithms use data from meteorological satellites, infrared imaging, and sensory data to predict and monitor wildfire intensity and progress. AI can analyze patterns in wind speed, temperature, humidity, and vegetation, which are often precursors to fire outbreaks.

6.2. Predictive Analytics for Disaster Preparedness

Predictive analytics is a revolutionary tool for disaster preparedness, providing us with insights into future disaster-prone areas. These insights help in designing and developing preparedness plans that foresee possible challenges, thereby enhancing the capacity of individuals and communities to anticipate, cope, and recover from potential disasters.

Using machine learning algorithms, historical disaster data is analyzed to identify patterns in terms of frequency, intensity, and geographical spread. For instance, AI algorithms scrutinise historical earthquake data and learn how different factors - seismic activity, plate tectonics, and geological structures - come together to cause an earthquake. Such models can give us early warnings for earthquakes, saving countless lives.

AI can also forecast climate change-induced floods. By analyzing precipitation data, river water level, soil moisture level, and topographical details, flood forecasting models can predict flooding events days, weeks, or even months in advance.

6.3. AI in Remote Sensing Data Analysis

High-quality remote sensing data is vital for disaster detection and response. AI plays a significant role in analyzing remote sensing data obtained from satellites. Deep learning algorithms analyze multispectral images captured by satellites to detect signs of disasters such as oil spills, fires, and cyclones in real time.

Using AI, we can even analyze how a disaster is progressing and assist rescue operations accordingly. For instance, during a cyclone, deep learning algorithms can constantly evaluate meteorological satellite data for changes in the storm's trajectory or intensity.

6.4. Disaster Impact Estimation and Resource Allocation

AI technologies not only help in detecting disasters but also in estimating their impact and the resources needed for effective response. Machine learning algorithms can analyze the extent of disaster-induced damage, providing insights into what kind of aid is needed and where.

AI models also play an essential role in informed disaster response strategy. By assessing the seriousness of the disaster and evaluating the affected population's needs, AI can help target resources optimally and decide the best rescue strategy. Machine-learning-based optimization models allocate resources such as food, shelter, medical aid, and rescue teams based on severity and needs on the ground.

6.5. Limitations and Ethical Considerations

While the applications of AI in disaster detection look promising, it does come with its own set of challenges. Data privacy is a significant concern, especially when AI algorithms use personal data to predict disasters. There's also a risk of data misinterpretation, given that AI learns from data provided. And then there's the problem of AI bias, where algorithms reflect the biases of their creators.

Therefore, as we utilize AI for disaster detection and management, it's crucial to consider these limitations and integrate ethical principles within the technology. Indeed, effective regulation and oversight can help ensure that AI is used responsibly, ensuring privacy, combating bias, and avoiding misinterpretation of data.

In conclusion, AI is a boon for disaster detection, with the potential to revolutionize the entire disaster management cycle. AI-powered disaster detection and management could save millions of lives, billions in property, and significantly reduce trauma and suffering. As we move forward and refine these technologies, we need to remember that these tools are not magic bullets. Instead, we must use them responsibly, ethically, and in conjunction with traditional disaster management strategies. AI is, after all, just a tool in our toolkit. If used correctly, it holds the potential to take disaster detection and response efforts to previously unimaginable heights.

Chapter 7. AI in Disaster Response: Automated and Enhanced Solutions

It's evident that modern crises demand modern solutions. With the advent of artificial intelligence (AI), disaster response mechanisms have potential to reap significant benefits from AI's ability to automate tasks, enhance operations, and effectively manage resources. Let's journey through an exploration of these capabilities.

7.1. Automation: The Catalyst to Streamline Operations

In a disaster response scenario, time is the most critical resource. AI's potential to automate operational tasks not only bolsters efficiency but opens up valuable time for strategists and first responders. Here are some instances of AI's transformative role:

1. Machine Learning (ML) algorithms have become adept at monitoring and detecting seismic activity, predicting weather changes, and analyzing trends that signify an impending disaster. These predictive models offer valuable time for preparatory measures.

2. AI-driven drones, combined with ML algorithms, can conduct an automated survey of an affected region. Equipped with high-resolution cameras and sensory data, they can detect survivors, identify hazards, and navigate inaccessible areas, a task impossible for humans.

3. Automation also brings efficiency in gathering information and filtering it. For instance, chatbots capable of understanding natural language can analyze incoming queries or reports from

affected individuals faster than human capabilities, thus keeping communication channels clear and efficient.

7.2. Enhanced Solutions: Revolutionizing Resilience and Reconstruction

AI's capabilities encompass more than automation alone. Enhanced AI solutions can improve resilience, orchestrate rehabilitation efforts, and ensure a smoother transition to the reconstruction stage. Here's how:

1. Intelligent evacuation route planning: AI algorithms can, in real-time, analyze the various constraints such as congestion and obstacles, provide optimized, dynamic evacuation routes for residents, and communicate these swiftly via mobile applications.

2. Predictive modelling for improved resilience: ML models can highlight infrastructural weaknesses, helping planners to design more resilient infrastructures, effectively "learning" from prior disasters to prevent similar damage in the future.

3. Robotic process automation (RPA) and AI can streamline relief coordination, managing donations, volunteers, supplies, and logistics, ensuring a seamless flow of aid for affected communities.

7.3. AI Intervention: Bringing Scalability and Precision in Resource Management

One of the significant challenges in disaster response is the allocation and management of resources. AI can revolutionize this aspect with precision and scalability:

1. AI algorithms can analyze and prioritize needs based on the dataset of affected regions, allowing authorities to distribute resources optimally.

2. Intelligent algorithms combined with IoT can assist in managing and scheduling emergency response vehicles, ensuring they reach the right place at the right time.

3. AI and geospatial technologies can accurately map the loss and damage, estimating the cost of exercise and facilitating insurance companies in precisely calculating the expenses.

7.4. Case Studies: Tangible Examples of AI in Disaster Response

While theoretical, the practical applications paint a clearer picture. Here are some instances where AI has been infused into disaster response:

1. Google's Flood Forecasting Initiative uses AI and computational hydrology to predict floods. Machine learning algorithms facilitate the delivery of accurate, timely flood warnings.

2. Following the 2019 Bahamas Hurricane Dorian, a training dataset of drone images was used to train an AI model. It successfully detected ruined buildings, roads, and areas with significant destruction.

3. Overstory, an environmental monitoring platform uses AI to understand and predict natural disasters by interpreting satellite and aerial imagery.

While we're still at the dawn of integrating AI completely into disaster management systems, these examples are exciting indicators of what lies ahead. With further research, implementation, training, and the right policies, AI stands poised to engulf disaster response mechanisms in its transformative wake. There is an urgent need for collaborative efforts from governments, technologists, and scientists. As we continue to navigate this embryonic field, the drive must be towards creating models that are ethical, transparent, accountable and robust, to ensure AI serves for the safety and wellbeing of all.

To conclude, the potential of AI in disaster response is tremendous, promising a future where we can better anticipate, respond and recover from disasters. It invites curiosity about the profound impact AI will have on human safety and wellbeing in the not-so-distant future.

Chapter 8. Mitigating Disaster Damage through AI

In the world of disaster response and management, the word "mitigation" signifies actions or steps that can minimize the impact of disasters. Traditionally, mitigation has been about developing and enforcing building codes, floodplain management, and organizing disaster education campaigns. However, with the emergence of AI, a fresh perspective on disaster mitigation has surfaced, offering potential to minimize risks, safeguard lives, and protect properties ahead of impending disasters.

8.1. Leveraging AI for Damage Prediction

AI's pivotal role begins with identifying and analyzing potential risk factors. By harnessing AI, we can predict potential damage zones, thereby enabling focused efforts towards reinforcing vulnerable areas or planning systematic evacuations.

Firstly, AI can compute massive data sets to identify patterns and trends. Weather data such as wind speed, rainfall, and temperature can be coupled with geographical data to predict the probable path and impact of disasters like hurricanes, floods, or wildfires. For example, IBM's 'Deep Thunder' combines machine learning, 3D modeling, and cloud computing to produce hyper-local weather forecasts in advance of catastrophes.

Secondly, AI can leverage satellites and remote sensing technology. Satellites like those from the European Space Agency's Copernicus Programme provide real-time images of Earth that can be processed using AI. This aids in detecting signs of environmental change which could indicate an imminent disaster.

Furthermore, the advent of Deep Learning has been transformative. Deep learning algorithms study satellite imagery to identify damage indicators like rubble or flooded areas, thereby offering a quantifiable measure of damage. By predicting future scenarios based on these measures, disaster mitigation strategies can be optimized.

8.2. AI in Disaster Mitigation Planning

Once areas of potential damage have been identified, AI can assist in formulating comprehensive mitigation strategies. AI algorithms can study past disasters and recovery efforts, housing codes, infrastructure health, and community resilience to create detailed and holistic mitigation plans.

Also, AI-driven simulations can test the robustness of these mitigation plans under various disaster scenarios. Multiple disaster simulations can be created and mitigation strategies can be improved iteratively based on their performance under these simulations. Some of these plans might include detailed evacuation routes, areas where housing codes need to be reinforced, and regions requiring upgraded infrastructure.

In order to make these plans accessible, AI can leverage Natural Language Processing (NLP) to translate complex mitigation strategies into simple and comprehensible guidelines. These guidelines, when delivered to authorities and communities via digital platforms, empower them to take proactive measures.

8.3. AI in Strengthening Infrastructure

AI's impact doesn't stop at planning. It's instrumental in implementing strategies by reinforcing existing infrastructure. AI systems can monitor the structural health of buildings and vital structures like bridges through sensor technology. Any signs of deterioration or need for repair can be proactively identified, enabling timely maintenance that can prevent exacerbated damage during disasters.

Moreover, AI embedded in design software can help architects and engineers create resilient constructions. For instance, AI can predict how buildings might resist or collapse under different disaster scenarios. This predictive capability can facilitate the construction of buildings that are not just safe for ordinary circumstances, but also robust against unpredicted catastrophic events.

8.4. Smart Emergency Response using AI

Disaster mitigation doesn't end with preventive measures. When disasters strike, prompt and efficient responses result in mitigating damage. Autonomous systems powered by AI, such as drones and robots, can be deployed in high-risk zones deemed too dangerous for human rescue teams. Drones can map areas quickly, facilitating faster rescue operations, while AI-powered amphibious robots can reach flood victims or detect underwater obstructions.

Telecommunication is key in such disaster-prone situations, and AI has a significant role here too. AI-based chatbots can quickly respond to thousands of queries simultaneously, providing distressed individuals with crucial information. Moreover, AI can streamline the operation of emergency hotlines, predict surge in call volumes and allocate resources accordingly.

To conclude, the advent of AI opens up myriad opportunities for disaster damage mitigation. By leveraging AI in predicting potential damage, devising robust mitigation strategies, strengthening disaster-prone infrastructure and facilitating efficient response in times of calamity, we can significantly minimize the detrimental impact of disasters. As AI continues to evolve, we can look forward to a future where disasters may still be inevitable, but their destruction doesn't have to be.

Chapter 9. Post-Disaster Recovery and AI: A Road to Rehabilitation

As we sweep over the debris and start patching the wounds, the relevance of a well-orchestrated strategy for rehabilitation becomes clear. Recovery and rehabilitation following a disaster are not singular projects. They are, instead, a series of complex processes that require diligent planning, efficient execution, and in-depth analysis. Even as conventional methods and protocols have played a significant role in managing post-disaster situations, the potential for leveraging artificial intelligence to augment these efforts is growing at an exponential pace.

9.1. AI-Enabled Damage Assessment

The first crucial step in post-disaster recovery is accurate damage assessment. Conventionally, this has always been a labor-intensive task. The physical inspection of the affected areas often takes several days, delaying the relief and recovery work, thus additionally burdening the community.

AI advancements now enable us to expedite the process by leveraging data obtained from satellite imagery, drones, or other remote sensing technologies. AI algorithms trained to recognize different types of buildings and infrastructure can, with high precision, assess the damage caused by a disaster. The speed and accuracy AI brings to the process are unparalleled, enabling quicker responses and ensuring aid is directed where it is most needed.

Furthermore, machine learning models can improve over time. As these models are exposed to more disaster scenarios, they learn and improve, thus providing a continuous learning mechanism that eventually enhances precision in damage assessment.

9.2. Smart Aid Distribution

Once the magnitude of the disaster is assessed, it is vital to ensure the right amount of aid reaches the correct locations swiftly. AI can play an indispensable role in optimizing aid distribution through predictive analytics. By analyzing data on affected areas and available resources, AI algorithms can provide insights on how to best allocate and distribute resources.

AI can also track real-time data from GPS fitted transport vehicles to ascertain the quickest and safest routes for resource transportation, taking into account aspects like road damage, traffic, and security issues. Apart from this, using pattern recognition and data from prior disasters, AI can predict delays or bottlenecks in the supply chain and help in formulating contingency plans.

9.3. Rebuilding Infrastructure

Restoring and rebuilding infrastructure is the backbone of any rehabilitation process. It starts with determining the priority of buildings and structures to be repaired or rebuilt. AI can analyze multiple factors like damage assessment data, importance of infrastructure (like hospitals or schools), and the number of people impacted to prioritize rebuilding efforts in a more structured and data-driven manner.

Additionally, AI can also play a pivotal role in creating resilient infrastructure. Machine learning can help in designing structures capable of withstanding future disasters based on pattern recognition from previous disasters. This, combined with predictive and simulation models, can help create disaster-resilient urban designs.

9.4. Socio-Economic Rehabilitation

While physical rebuilding is crucial, socio-economic rehabilitation is often the tougher task at hand. After the initial phase of arranging food, shelter, and medical care subsides, the communities face economic hardships, job loss, and post-traumatic stress. Here too, AI can lend a helping hand.

AI-powered skill mapping can recommend alternative employment opportunities based on a person's skill set. In addition, AI-enabled psychometric tests can be used to screen for mental health issues. AI systems can subsequently suggest personalized therapy routines that make optimal use of available resources, thus ensuring an appropriate mental health response.

9.5. Policy Assistance for Aid

AI's potential for identifying recurring patterns in disaster scenarios can significantly assist policy planning. Policies regarding disaster management can be reviewed and updated based on trends and predictions provided by AI systems. This proactive approach to policy reform can ensure that laws remain relevant and efficient, even in rapidly changing circumstances.

Addressing post-disaster recovery with the relentless assistance of Artificial Intelligence is not just a matter of feasibility; it is the way forward. By merging human ingenuity with machine intelligence, we can create a robust and resilient system that puts people first in the wake of disasters. The road to rehabilitation will indeed be long and arduous, but with AI as our ally, we can make the journey a little less challenging.

Chapter 10. Case Studies: Successful AI Deployment in Disaster Management

Though we can't provide full 5 A4 pages content here due to character limitations, let's dive deep into some engaging case studies that demonstrate how the deployment of AI can transform disaster management.

10.1. AI in Earthquake Early Warning Systems: Mexico

In the world's most seismically active region, Mexico City, SkyAlert, a seismic alert company uses machine learning algorithms to provide early earthquake warnings. Its system, equipped with hundreds of sensors across the country, uses AI to decode seismic activity metrics and provide citizens with life-saving prior warnings. The algorithm evaluates the data and depending on the type, location, and magnitude of detected earthquakes, decides whether or not to send an alert.

In 2017, when an earthquake of magnitude 7.1 hit central Mexico, SkyAlert's AI-driven warning system sparked notices to millions of users before the earthquake's waves could have devastating effects. Thus, the technology helped in enabling rapid evacuation procedures and mitigating life-threatening situations.

10.2. AI in Flood Forecasting: India

In 2018, Google's AI-based flood forecasting initiative started in India, driven by machine learning techniques to predict flood occurrences, particularly in the monsoon-stressed region of Patna. Utilizing elevation and satellite maps, real-time rainfall patterns, and a host of historical events of flooding, this AI model provided vital alerts and inundation maps to locals.

This advance warning system assisted locals in embarking on mitigation activities faster, which is especially crucial considering the speed and potential damage capacity of flash floods. In 2019, Google was able to alert thousands of individuals in advance of Cyclone Fani, which left them ample time for preparatory activities.

10.3. AI in Wildfire Prediction: USA

The United States, particularly California, faces a recurring wildfire crisis. To combat this, the AI-powered application, "Wildfire Analyst", uses massive sets of historical climate data, current weather conditions, details about vegetation, and topographical information to predict wildfire spread patterns.

The AI model not only forecasts the path and intensity of the fires but also provides insights on how changing weather conditions might affect the fire's propagation. Wildfire Analyst's accurate real-time predictions allow fire departments to strategize firefighting resources to areas of imminent threat, subsequently saving lives, properties, and vast expanses of flora and fauna.

10.4. Conclusion

Accentuating Mexico's SkyAlert, Google's flood prediction system in India, or Wildfire Analyst in the US, these AI implementations in disaster management provide compelling cases of AI aiding disaster mitigation efforts. By emulating these examples, new horizons of AI applications in disaster management could be discovered worldwide. The effectiveness of AI lies in understanding its proficiency, and the realm of its implementation. It is high time that policy-makers, governments, and stakeholders take inspiration from these cases and shape the strategies for AI adoption in their regions.

Chapter 11. The Future of Disaster Management: AI and Beyond

The integration of Artificial Intelligence (AI) in our daily lives has improved efficiency across various sectors. Now, it's playing a pivotal role in shaping our responses to disasters - from early warning systems to disaster recovery. This bold new approach could redefine the way we manage and recover from catastrophes.

11.1. AI for Early Warning and Risk Prediction

The heart of any disaster management framework lies in being capable of predicting and providing warnings beforehand. AI can effectively optimize this by assessing risk factors and predicting impending disasters with remarkable accuracy. Machine learning algorithms, a subfield of AI, process historical and real-time data from various sources, like weather patterns, seismic signals, satellite imagery, and more, to predict natural disasters such as cyclones, earthquakes, or floods.

AI's predictive ability doesn't just stop with natural calamities; it is also capable of predicting man-made disasters by scanning social media for anomalies and assessing data from law enforcement databases. AI algorithms help in the recognition of forewarning signs, thus enabling authorities to take preemptive steps.

11.2. Using AI for Evacuation Planning

Once a threat has been identified, the next crucial step is to implement a well-coordinated evacuation plan. Traditional evacuation strategies often fail to consider unique circumstances that could hinder or complicate the evacuation process. AI and machine learning, however, can analyze both big picture trends and individual factors to enhance evacuation plans.

Through data-driven models, AI can simulate various disaster and evacuation scenarios, providing decision-makers with real-time situational information. Authorities can leverage AI to identify optimal evacuation routes by evaluating parameters like size of the population, available transportation, and the condition of road networks. This can reduce congestion during evacuations, ultimately ensuring the safety of people.

11.3. AI in Disaster Response

Notably, AI's involvement in disaster management is not just restricted to pre-disaster scenarios. It also assists with post-disaster management and recovery efforts. After a disaster, AI can streamline information collection efforts by automating the analysis of photographs and drone videos. Machine learning applications can detect damaged roads, bridges, buildings, and other key infrastructures.

In the face of a burgeoning surge of information during a disaster, AI can use Natural Language Processing (NLP) to analyze social media data and texts, helping to identify and locate those in need of immediate aid.

AI's role in disaster response extends to the management of aid and supplies too. AI algorithms can parse through a large amount of data to predict where aid will be needed the most, crucial for efficient, timely distribution of resources.

11.4. Long-term Recovery and Rehabilitation Enabled by AI

AI can also aid in the long-term recovery process by providing an analytical framework to assess damage and predict future needs. Drone footage or satellite image analysis could help in determining the scale and scope of infrastructural damage, consequently leading to a comprehensive and well-strategized rehabilitation plan.

AI can help us understand patterns of how communities rebuild, enabling policy makers to create data-driven strategies for allocation of resources. This could result in more resilient infrastructures and better-prepared communities, enhancing our ability to cope with future disasters.

11.5. Ethical Considerations and Challenges of AI in Disaster Management

While AI presents many opportunities for disaster management, it is crucial to consider the accompanying ethical concerns and potential pitfalls. Issues of privacy, data ownership, and the risk of creating AI that reflects or amplifies existing inequalities and biases are legitimate concerns that need to be addressed.

Moreover, the over-reliance on AI could potentially lead to complacency in decision-making, diminishing the critical human aspect in disaster management. AI should be seen as a tool that augments human ability, not as a replacement.

11.6. Concluding Remarks

The leaps and bounds made in AI technology present monumental potential for disaster management and recovery in the years to come. Even with the challenges and concerns, the reality is that the marriage of AI and disaster management could save countless lives and resources in the future.

At its core, the deployment of AI in disaster management reaffirms a fundamental truth – technology, when thoughtfully implemented, can greatly enhance our ability to face our most daunting challenges. Infusing AI technology in disaster management plans offers the promise of a future where communities are more resilient and better prepared in the face of any adversity.

www.ingramcontent.com/pod-product-compliance
Lightning Source LLC
Chambersburg PA
CBHW071040260726
48661CB00007B/3087